SMART Board® Lessons:
Narrative Writing

40 Ready-to-Use, Motivating Lessons on CD to Help You
Teach Essential Writing Skills

W9-CNA-883

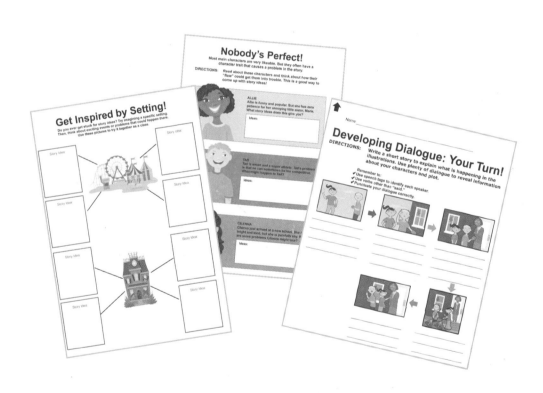

by Karen Kellaher

New York • Toronto • London • Auckland • Sydney
Mexico City • New Delhi • Hong Kong • Buenos Aires

Teaching Resources

For Diana Mai, one of the SMART-est teachers I know.

Text © 2010 by Karen M. Kellaher

Edited by Maria L. Chang and Betsy Pringle

Illustrations by Kelly J. Brownlee

Cover design by Brian Larossa

Designed by Rosanna Brockley

Design assistance by Richard Anderson and Tyler Freidenrich

Production by Jennifer Marx

SMART Board® Lessons: Narrative Writing
is produced by **becker&mayer!**, Bellevue, WA 98004

ISBN-13: 978-0-545-14026-3

ISBN-10: 0-545-14026-9

10296

Printed, manufactured, and assembled in Hong Kong, China 11/09.

2 3 4 5 6 7 8 9 10   15 14 13 12 11 10

Contents

Introduction

Not long ago, I mentioned to a brilliant retired teacher I know how much I was enjoying creating lessons fo the SMART Board. "Smart what?" was her puzzled response. Though she has been out of the classroom for only six years, she had never heard of—much less used—an interactive whiteboard. Now, a typical school in our area has a huge SMART Board in the computer lab and an equally huge teacher waiting list for the portable units available for classroom use.

That conversation illustrated for me just how fast the technology landscape is changing in our schools. Alm as fast as you can say, "Budget approved," SMART Boards and similar whiteboard units are replacing overhe projectors and "old-fashioned" dry-erase boards. There are several excellent reasons why.

- The SMART Board offers instant lesson engagement. Whether you are teaching about nouns, narratives, or Roman numerals, you will have students' immediate attention. Many of today's kids were computer literate even before they started school. They are accustomed to games and gadgets that respond to the touch of a fingertip. A SMART Board grabs their attention in a way that blackboards and handouts fail to do.

- Because it offers a large, interactive display and opportunities for collaborative learning, the SMART Board is a smart way to teach students 21st-century skills like working in teams, marking text electronically, synthesizing information, organizing data, interpreting visual aids, and evaluating Web sites. These skills are an increasingly important part of the standards in many states.

- The SMART Board is easy to use, even for technophobes. I didn't believe it myself (in fact, I was a little scared of the giant whiteboard) until I took my first workshop. But, using the board and the accompanying Notebook software is fairly intuitive. On the interactive whiteboard, you can do anything you can do on your computer screen—and then some. So, even if you are just learning the technology, you can pull off a fun, effective lesson.

About the CD and Book

Make the most of SMART technology within your language arts curriculum. The SMART Notebook pages on the CD are a perfect way to teach writing skills because they allow you to model concepts and skills for the whole class. You can read and analyze pieces of text together, deciding what works and why. You can move, highlight, underline, and change text right on the whiteboard. And, best of all, you can save *everythi* for later use or review. When your class comes up with awesome sensory details or alternatives to replace the dreaded *said,* you can capture the discussion on screen using our organizers and activities, then provide students with copies for their writing folders.

The CD contains five units on narrative writing skills. Each unit is a Notebook file with eight interactive pa that take advantage of the SMART technology without being overwhelming to the SMART Board novice. Yo find opportunities to use the Creative Pens, on-screen keyboard, graphic organizers, cloning tools, drag-and drop feature, and more. Instructions for using each SMART tool are embedded in the lesson plans.

ch unit on the CD introduces narrative writing skills in a gradual-release format. The first lesson in each
it introduces the topic, engages students' attention, and establishes what they already know. In the next
lessons, students collaboratively explore concrete skills related to the topic. In the last "lesson," students
thesize and apply what they have learned in a brief independent writing assignment. You may choose to
ve students complete this final Your Turn! activity in class or as a homework assignment.

is book contains easy-to-use lessons corresponding to each CD unit. Lessons include objectives, pacing
ggestions, and step-by-step directions for teaching with each SMART Notebook page on the CD. They also
rrelate with important language arts standards.

ch Tips

hough the SMART Writing CD was created using Notebook 10 software, you will be able to use the
ivities with older versions of the software. If you are still getting the hang of your SMART Board, be sure
look for the technology tips offered at various points throughout the units. However, the following
an overview of the main Notebook features you will be using.

SMART Pens These are the black, red, green, and blue pens that came with your SMART Board.
Use them to write directly on the screen in digital ink.

Creative Pens A student favorite, this tool allows you to draw fun lines made of smiley faces, stars,
rainbow stripes, and more.

Magic Pen When students circle text or art with the Magic Pen, a spotlight focuses on the circled
portion of the page. Everything else on the page goes dark temporarily. It's a dramatic way to focus
attention on one element on a page!

Eraser Like its old-fashioned counterparts, this eraser removes unwanted writing. It will work on text
and lines created with the SMART pens. It will not work on typed text or art objects.

On-Screen Keyboard If your students are adding text to a small field or simply prefer typing to
writing freehand, use the on-screen keyboard. You can access it by touching the keyboard icon on
the front tray of your SMART Board.

Properties Tool In several of the activities in this book, you will be guided to use this feature to
change the color or style of a SMART pen or to add color to a box.

Screen Shade A teacher favorite, this tool allows you to cover part of a page while focusing attention
on another part. Activate the shade by clicking on the Screen Shade icon on your toolbar. Deactivate
it by clicking again. To gradually open a shade that covers your screen, use one of the circular buttons
on the shade itself to drag the shade open.

Designing Settings

A strong setting invites readers into a story and plays a significant role in shaping the plot. Use this series of Notebook pages to introduce the narrative "when" and "where" and to help students develop strong settings in their own writing.

OBJECTIVES

Students will be able to:

✓ Understand the main components of setting (time and place).

✓ Use setting to generate story ideas.

✓ Use sensory details to describe various story settings.

TIME

About 3–4 class periods for Unit 1 (allow 15–20 minutes per lesson)

MEETING THE STANDARDS

This lesson correlates with the following writing standards for grades 3 through 6

- Students identify and describe all aspects of the setting of a story (e.g., time of day, place, year).

- Students generate ideas using organizers and other prewriting strategie

- Students write narratives using concrete sensory details.

GETTING READY

Before students arrive, have your SMART Board ready to go. Load the Writing Lessons CD onto your host computer and copy the 1 SMART Settings Notebook file onto your hard drive. Open the local file. The first interactive page, *Exploring Story Settings*, will appear on your SMART Board. If you wish, use your Screen Shade tool to conceal the page until you are ready to begin.

ploring Story Settings

Display *Exploring Story Settings* on the SMART Board. To begin, ask students to think about what we mean by *setting*. Solicit definitions from the class. You may find that students think initially of the geographic aspect of setting, that is, *where* a story takes place. Guide them to understand that setting also includes another important "W"—*when* the story takes place. Explain that both the geographic and temporal aspects of setting can play a huge role in a story, determining how characters behave, the problems they encounter, and how they tackle those problems.

Invite students to think of some stories they have read recently. For each example, record the book title on the graphic organizer. (Use a SMART pen or the on-screen keyboard to write text directly on the organizer.) Then ask students to share where and when the narrative took place. Have students record these setting details in the text boxes of the organizer.

💡 TECH TIP

If students have trouble writing with the SMART pens, check that they are holding the stylus correctly. If a student's wrist or hand rubs against the screen while writing, his or her writing will appear garbled and illegible. When using these pens, only the stylus tip should make contact with the SMART Board.

Use students' examples to make the following points:

- **What we know about setting can vary greatly from book to book.** Some authors offer specific details about setting, but others prefer to leave place names and dates up to the reader's imagination. For example, in *Journey to America* by Sonia Levitin, we are told that the action takes place in 1938 in Berlin, Germany. However, in *Sarah, Plain and Tall* by Patricia MacLachlan, no town, state, or year is specified. We know simply that the story takes place in the American prairie in a time when horse-drawn carriages were a main form of transportation. Both techniques can be very effective.

- **Setting has many layers.** Place can involve a country, state, city, neighborhood, building, or even room. Time might include historical era, year, season, month, day of the week, or time of day.

Save your class's graphic organizer. Later, make a copy for each student to keep in his or her writing folder.

Map It Out

1. Display *Map It Out* on the SMART Board. Point out that authors often vary th setting within a story in order to move the plot along. For example, a charact might have a problem at school during the day, then go home to discuss solutions with his parents.

2. If time permits, read aloud a short story with several small settings within on general setting. As you read, ask students to note each time a new location is introduced. Below are some examples of picture books that are perfect for th purpose. If time is tight, you might prefer to have students retell a well-know fairy tale, such as "Cinderella," and take note of the locations within the tale.

Pinduli

by Janell Cannon

A young hyena earns some respect.

General setting:
East African scrublands

Places: water hole, brush, ridge, canyon, hyena den

Thunder Cake

by Patricia Polacco

A girl and her grandma bake to ease anxiety during a storm.

General setting:
farm in Michigan

Places: farmhouse, barn, dry shed, woods, barnyard

The True Story of the Three Little Pigs

by Jon Scieszka

Alexander T. Wolf explains that he was framed.

General setting:
fairy-tale neighborhood

Places: Wolf's home, house of straw, house of sticks, house of bricks, jail cell

---

TECH TIP

To clone, click on the item, then click on the small downward arrow that appears at the top right corner of the item. On the menu that appears, select Clone. A duplicate text box will appear next to the original. You can repeat as often as needed.

3. Direct students' attention to the Notebook page. Use your black SMART pen to jot down the story title in the blue box. Then, invite students to recall important locations within the story. Create a text box for each location by "cloning" the text box in the Map Key.

4. Write the place names in the text boxes. Then, move the boxes to desired spo on the map template. If your story includes a body of water, you might want to clone the blue line on the Map Key or draw a blue line or circle yourself. To add a line, use your blue SMART pen, clicking on the Properties side tab thicken the line.

5. Have students identify the location where most of the action takes place. Lab it with a star. (Clone the star from the Map Key or select a star under Shapes on your toolbar.)

6. Save your class's work and make a copy for each student's writing folder.

About Time!

Display *It's About Time!* on the SMART Board. Make sure the Screen Shade is activated. The Screen Shade should cover the right side of the page, leaving the page title and left column open to view.

Explain that the time when a story takes place is just as important as the place where it happens. In fact, the timing helps to determine the story's genre. Discuss with students that narrative genres include historical fiction, contemporary realistic fiction, science fiction, and others.

Direct students' attention to the left side of the Notebook page and have them read aloud the descriptions of the three genres. Next, open the Screen Shade and read the blurbs about the three imaginary books in the column on the right.

Starting with Contemporary Fiction, discuss which book title matches each genre. Then have students "draw" lines to connect the matches. Students may enjoy selecting a Creative Pen from your toolbar to create their lines. Once a Creative Pen is selected, they can use a finger to click and drag the line from one column to the other.

Have students share with the class the clues that they used to make each match. Use prompts if necessary. For example, ask: *How do you know that* Homesick *is set in the future? What words in the summary of* My Friend Moanam *suggest that it is set long ago?* Use a regular SMART pen to underline the clues that students share.

Encourage students to think about each genre from a writer's perspective. Ask: *What would you need to know in order to set a story long ago?* (What buildings looked like, what people wore, etc.) *How would you find out?* (Research) *What would you need to know to set your story in the future?* (The same things) *How could you decide?* (Use your imagination) Guide students to understand that each kind of setting places different demands on the writer.

If time permits, have students name other stories they have read for each of the three time-linked genres.

Save your class's work and make a copy for each student's writing folder.

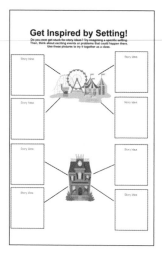

Get Inspired by Setting!

1. Display *Get Inspired by Setting!* on the SMART Board. Ask students to raise th hands if they have ever been stumped for a story idea. Explain that one way to generate great story ideas is to picture a particular setting—a classroom, ballet studio, or a baseball stadium, for example—and imagine the kinds of problems a person could encounter there. (Remind students that narratives built around a problem/conflict and solution/resolution.)

2. Have students look at the first graphic organizer on the screen. Invite them describe the setting. (Depending on where you live, students might interpre the setting as a carnival, fair, or amusement park.) Then ask students what kinds of conflicts or problems they imagine might happen there. Use the ci of the idea web to record their ideas.

3. Scroll down and repeat the activity for the second setting (a haunted-lookin house). Encourage students to consider the time of day. Then have them ag imagine what sorts of conflicts or problems might happen here. They can also use their imaginations to decide what historical era and time of year ea photo depicts.

4. Point out that students can draw their own setting idea webs to gather ideas during the prewriting phase of the writing process. In the center circle, they can use a photo from a magazine or newspaper, sketch a setting, or write a short description of a setting.

5. Save your class's work and make a copy for each student's writing folder.

ss the Setting

Display *Guess the Setting* on the SMART Board. Have on hand the setting clues for this game. (Clues are on page 12.) Guide students to understand that authors often use sensory details to describe a setting. Such details are a wonderful way to paint a picture in readers' minds. To illustrate, work with students to describe your classroom using all five senses.

Tell students that you are going to play a game to see how well they can use sensory details to guess a setting. For this game, students will focus on the place aspect of setting.

Divide the class into two teams. Have each team choose a color and a spokesperson. Ask two student volunteers to help you "host" the game. One will read the clues and the other will update the game board as teams win points.

Review the rules of the game.

RULES

- The goal is to guess the setting as quickly as possible. Teams take turns choosing setting squares on the board. They will earn 3 points for naming a setting with the first clue they are given, 2 points for naming the setting with the second clue, and 1 point for naming it with the last clue.

- A team can give one guess per clue and will have 30 seconds of brainstorming time per clue. During that time, they may talk freely.

- Only the team spokesperson may officially give answers.

- If a team is unable to guess the setting after the third and final clue, the other team gets a chance to guess. If the other team is correct, they earn 1 point. That team gets to choose the next square, regardless of the outcome of the preceding turn.

Flip a coin to determine which team will go first. The first team should begin play by choosing a square on the board. Read the corresponding clue. After 30 seconds, ask the team spokesperson for the team's answer. If they do not have an answer, read the second and third clues, pausing in between for the team to answer if they wish.

As a team correctly names a setting, type the number of points they earned in the square (or have a student volunteer do so). Then, shade the box to match the team's chosen color.

Once all the boxes have been filled (or at any point once both teams have had an equal number of turns), determine the winner. Count the number of points each team earned. The team with the most points wins.

Save your class's work.

TECH TIP

To shade a box, click on the box to be shaded and then click on the Properties side tab ▦A . Select Fill Effects, and choose a color.

Clues for "Guess the Setting"

Setting 1

Clue 1: A drill whines softly in the background. (*3 points*)

Clue 2: People fidget nervously in chairs along the wall. (*2 points*)

Clue 3: A poster called "Caring for Your Teeth" hangs on the wall. (*1 point*)

*Answer: **Dentist's office***

Setting 2

Clue 1: Bright lights hang over the crowded aisles. (*3 points*)

Clue 2: Colorful cans and boxes line the shelves. (*2 points*)

Clue 3: People push carts. (*1 point*)

*Answer: **Grocery store***

Setting 3

Clue 1: Men and women in suits check their watches and look down a dark corridor. (*3 points*)

Clue 2: Suitcases sit on the concrete floor. (*2 points*)

Clue 3: A rumbling noise grows louder and louder. (*1 point*)

*Answer: **Train station***

Setting 4

Clue 1: People speak in hushed voices. (*3 points*)

Clue 2: You hear the turning of pages and the click of a computer keyboard. (*2 points*)

Clue 3: There are books as far as the eye can see. (*1 point*)

*Answer: **Library***

Setting 5

Clue 1: The aroma of taco meat fills the room. (*3 points*)

Clue 2: You hear laughter and conversation. (*2 points*)

Clue 3: Kids carry plastic trays. (*1 point*)

*Answer: **School cafeteria***

Setting 6

Clue 1: The smell of hay tickles your nose. (*3 points*)

Clue 2: A horse neighs and whinnies. (*2 points*)

Clue 3: A tractor hums nearby. (*1 point*)

*Answer: **Farm***

Setting 7

Clue 1: Sneakers squeak on a shiny floor. (*3 points*)

Clue 2: Spectators clap and cheer. (*2 points*)

Clue 3: A ball bounces rhythmically. (*1 point*)

*Answer: **Basketball court***

Setting 8

Clue 1: Brightly colored towels line the grass and pavement. (*3 points*)

Clue 2: The scent of chlorine drifts through the air. (*2 points*)

Clue 3: You hear a big splash. (*1 point*)

*Answer: **Pool***

Setting 9

Clue 1: Little children run and laugh. (*3 points*)

Clue 2: You take a deep breath of fresh air. (*2 points*)

Clue 3: A swing squeaks as it sways back and forth. (*1 point*)

*Answer: **Playground***

Setting 10

Clue 1: Sunlight peeks through the leaves. (*3 points*)

Clue 2: A squirrel scurries across your path. (*2 points*)

Clue 3: You hear twigs snap and leaves crunch under your feet. (*1 point*)

*Answer: **Woods or forest***

Setting 11

Clue 1: Pale sand stretches as far as the eye can see. (*3 points*)

Clue 2: A brown lizard rests on a rock. (*2 points*)

Clue 3: You feel the prickly spines of a cactus plant. (*1 point*)

*Answer: **Desert***

Setting 12

Clue 1: People carry bundles of envelopes. (*3 points*)

Clue 2: Blue metal boxes line the wall. (*2 points*)

Clue 3: A long line forms near a glass window. (*1 point*)

*Answer: **Post office***

Display *Learn From the Pros* on the SMART Board. Share with students that many famous stories begin with a description of setting. The author paints a mental picture of the setting by engaging some or all of the senses. Explain that these are called *sensory details*.

Tell students that they will read two story beginnings that describe setting, then identify the details that tell what someone would see, hear, taste, smell, or feel. Draw students' attention to the first example, the beginning of *Owl Moon* by Jane Yolen. Have students read aloud the two versions and vote on which one they prefer. Use a SMART Creative Pen to put a check by the preferred text.

Now have students look closely at the green box that contains the real story beginning. Invite them to search for words and phrases that appeal to the senses. When a student spots a sensory detail, have him or her use a SMART highlighter to mark it.

Repeat until students have highlighted all of the sensory details in the passage. *(No wind; trees stood still as giant statues; moon was so bright the sky seemed to shine; train whistle blew . . . like a sad, sad song)*

Repeat with the opening of *Harry Potter and the Order of the Phoenix*. Again, have students use a finger to highlight the sensory details. *(Hottest day of summer; drowsy silence; large, square houses; cars . . . stood dusty; lawns . . . parched and yellowing; windows thrown wide; teenage boy who was lying flat on his back)*

Guide students to notice which senses are engaged in the two beginnings. *(Both appeal to sight, touch, and hearing.)* Challenge students to imagine a detail they could add to either story opening that shows what someone might taste or smell.

Save your class's work and make a copy for each student's writing folder.

TECH TIP

To access a highlighter, have the student use a finger to click on the SMART pens icon, then select the wide yellow line style. The student can now drag a finger over the desired text to highlight it.

TECH TIP

If highlighting or underline marks don't show up exactly where you want them, it's probably a sign that your SMART Board needs to be reoriented. Orienting ensures that your board is properly aligned. It is especially important to reorient if you are using a portable SMART Board unit. To orient, look on the Notebook software's startup menu.

Revise for Setting

1. Display *Revise for Setting* on the SMART Board. As you enter this Notebook page, have students pay close attention to the screen. Icons representing the five senses will fly onto the page! Use this animation as an opportunity to remind students of what they have already learned about using sensory details. Explain to students that it's time for them to try their own hand at this author's craft.

2. Read the directions together, explaining that students will revise a boring story opening by adding sensory details to engage readers. Review the specific color ink to use for each type of sensory detail.

3. Read the story opening together and allow a few minutes for students to brainstorm sensory details. Then invite students to share their details with the class and add them to the text box on the screen. For red, blue, and green ink, students can simply pick up one of the SMART pens from the pen tray on the front of your SMART Board and begin writing.

4. Read aloud the story beginning with the sensory details that students have added. Discuss how the revision improved the writing.

5. Save your class's work and make a copy for each student's writing folder.

TECH TIP

For the other two colors, pick up the black SMART pen and go to the Properties icon. Select line style. Choose the appropriate color (purple for smell or orange for taste) from the color palette. Go back to the Notebook page and begin writing. The black pen will temporarily have orange or purple "ink."

EXTENDED LEARNING

Designing Settings: Your Turn!

1. Print and make copies of *Designing Settings: Your Turn!* for students. Display the Notebook page on the SMART Board. Distribute copies of the worksheet. Explain that students will complete this page on their own, either in class or for homework, to apply what they have learned about story settings.

2. Review the directions with students, explaining that they will create a picture postcard for a setting of their choice. Remind students to:
    • choose a setting they think will inspire great stories and draw or paste an image of that setting on the card.
    • include both place and time in their setting descriptions.
    • appeal to all five senses in a description of their setting.

3. Invite volunteers to share their work with the class.

Creating Characters

his series of interactive Notebook pages, students study examples of
l-developed characters and learn how to make their own characters
ne alive through description, dialogue, and action.

BJECTIVES

dents will be able to:

✓ Distinguish between main and supporting characters.

✓ Recognize techniques for developing characters, including
descriptions of appearance and personality, internal and external
dialogue, and the reactions of other characters.

✓ Understand how a character's flaws contribute to a narrative.

✓ Write a character sketch to create an original main character.

ME

ut 3–4 class periods for Unit 2 (allow 15–20 minutes per lesson)

EETING THE STANDARDS

s lesson correlates with the following writing standards for grades 3 through 6:

• Students analyze the use of literary elements by an author,
including characterization.

• Students distinguish between direct and indirect
characterization.

• Students identify and describe characters' physical traits,
basic personality traits, and actions.

ETTING READY

ore students arrive, have your SMART Board ready to go. Load the Writing
sons CD onto your host computer and copy the 2 SMART Characters
tebook file onto your hard drive. Open the local file. The first interactive
e, *What a Character!*, will appear on your SMART Board. If you wish, use
r Screen Shade tool 🖳 to conceal the page until you are ready to begin.

INTRODUCING THE CONCEPT

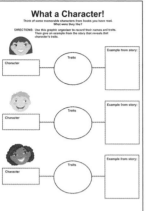

What a Character!

1. Display *What a Character!* on the SMART Board and use it to tap into student prior knowledge of story characters. Review the parts of the graphic organizer. Explain that a *trait* is a quality or characteristic that describes someone. Give two or three examples of traits, then check understanding by asking students to name some others. Encourage them to think beyond physical descriptors.

Examples of Character Traits

funny	caring	grumpy
brave	selfish	curious
smart	honest	lazy
mischievous	mean	adventurous

2. Invite students to think of some memorable characters in children's literature. Model what you expect students to do by sharing one of your own favorite characters with the class. For example, you might say:

    I think Max from Where the Wild Things Are *is one of the most memorable characters I have ever encountered. One trait that makes him so memorable is his incredible imagination. In the book, he thinks up a whole pretend setting, full of odd monsters, where he can be in charge.*

3. Record the characters, traits, and examples on the organizer. If students have difficulty backing up their traits with examples, ask, *"How do you <u>know</u> that this character is smart (or adventurous, or funny, or whatever the trait may be)?"* If you are using the SMART pens, have students write directly on the graphic organizer. If you prefer to use the on-screen keyboard, push the keyboard button on your pen tray to make the keyboard appear on your screen. Don't hesitate to "recycle" the organizers by erasing your digital ink or typing over previous text.

4. Guide students to understand that we remember these characters because the author worked hard to make them come alive for us. Explain that in this unit, students will learn how to accomplish that in their own writing.

If students name characters from series (such as the well-meaning but mischievous Junie B. Jones or the adventure-seeking Harry Potter), point out that a successful series is often a sign of a well-developed character. The author writes one book based on the character, and readers clamor for more! Have students name other strong characters around whom series have been built.

Save your class's work and make a copy for each student's writing folder.

TECH TIP

When using the SMART pens to add text to a page, try out the handwriting-recognition feature of your SMART Board. Simply click on the handwritten word(s) and go to the arrow in the upper right-hand corner for a pull-down menu. Select "Recognize as (correct word)." To boost accuracy, make sure handwritten letters are not too far apart.

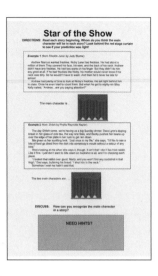

Star of the Show

1. Display *Star of the Show* on the SMART Board. Guide students to understand that a main character is the most important person in the story. It is the character around whom the action takes place. Explain that most stories have one main character. A few have two main characters who solve a problem together. (Jack and Annie in the Magic Tree House series are a great example

2. Explain that other characters may be important to the story and interesting to readers. They may be friends or family members of the main character, people who cause a problem for the main character, or strangers whom the main character encounters. They are called *secondary* or supporting characte Explain that an author does not spend as much time or effort telling us abou these characters as he or she does introducing the main character.

3. Tell students they are going to read the beginnings of two books and try to predict whom the main character(s) will be. Read aloud the first excerpt, fro Judy Blume's *Freckle Juice*. Invite students to predict which character will be the main character and to back up their predictions with evidence from the text. Use the SMART pens to underline the clues students used to make thei prediction.

> ### Examples
>
> Students may offer evidence like the following:
>
> - *His is the first name mentioned.*
> - *There is a lot of information about him.*
> - *She's the one telling the story.*

4. Tell students that it's now time to see if their prediction was right. Have a student volunteer approach the SMART Board and use a finger to tap on the image of the stage curtain. The curtain will "open" (fly off the page) and t main character's name (Andrew Marcus) will be revealed.

5. Direct students' attention to the second text box. This is the beginning of Phyllis Reynolds Naylor's award-winning novel *Shiloh*. Let students know th this one is challenging because Naylor introduces many characters right off the bat. Repeat the predicting activity, again discussing and recording the cl students used to guess the main character. Point out that the prompt under the text box reveals an important clue: This story has two main characters. Y may wish to share that one of the main characters is not human.

6. Have a student volunteer touch the stage curtain to reveal the main characte of *Shiloh*. They are Marty, the narrator, and Shiloh, a dog.

Use the discussion question at the bottom of the Notebook page to review some of the ways to identify a main character. Then drag the "Need Hints?" box away from its spot for a list of ways to recognize main characters. Compare this list to the ideas that emerged during your discussion.

- The main character is introduced at or near the beginning of the story.

- We are told what is going on inside the main character's head. We know what he or she is thinking and feeling. (We don't know what the other characters think, only what they say out loud.)

- The main character is sometimes (but not always) the one telling the story. This is called the *narrator*.

- The main character is the one facing the problem or challenge in the story.

- The name of the main character is sometimes in the story title.

Save your class's work and make a copy for each student's writing folder.

...ect or Indirect?

Display *Direct or Indirect?* on the SMART Board and read the introductory material together. Pay special attention to the examples of direct and indirect characterization. Ask students which example better catches their attention and which technique they'd like to use to describe characters in their own writing.

Guide students to understand that in most stories, authors use both techniques. For example, a writer may use direct characterization first ("Jason was the class clown"), then follow it up with indirect characterization ("He never stopped cracking jokes and slipping off his chair").

Scroll down to the chart beneath the examples. Have students work together to fill in the parts that are missing. The first entry provides an indirect characterization of a character named Stephen. Read this text aloud and ask students if they can think of a direct way of describing Stephen, perhaps using the prompt "Stephen was a _____." Possible responses include *bully* and *jerk*.

Explore the second entry together. In this one, the character Stella is directly described as a teacher's pet. Challenge students to brainstorm ways of describing Stella as a teacher's pet indirectly. Does Stella raise her hand for every answer? Does she get special treatment? Let students' imaginations run wild. Have students use the SMART pens to enter a few favorite details in the indirect characterization column.

If time permits, have student pairs look through books in your classroom library for examples of direct and indirect characterization. Have pairs share with the class.

Save your class's work and make a copy for each student's writing folder.

Character Clues

1. Display *Character Clues, Part 1,* and *Character Clues, Part 2* on the SMART Board. Use the Split Screen tool 🖵 to display both pages at once.

2. Explain that students are going to further explore ways in which authors can develop characters. Point out that the screen now holds two pages. One is a short story students will read together, paying special attention to what they can learn about the main character. The other is a chart they will complete using details from the story.

3. Click on the split-screen icon again to return to a single-screen format. Look at the chart (Part 2) first in order to set a purpose and context for reading. Have students read the chart directions and the headings. Make sure students understand that, as they read, they will be looking for details about Bianca's appearance, speech, actions, and private thoughts, as well as other characters' reactions to her.

4. Display the short story and read it aloud (or, if you prefer, provide printed copies for students to read at their seats). Divide the class into small groups find and discuss examples of character development.

5. After a few minutes, bring the class back together to complete the chart on the SMART Board. Invite each group to share one favorite example of how the writer developed Bianca's character. A group representative can use a SMART pen to record the example in the second column of the chart. Discuss what each detail tells about Bianca, and have another group representative record that revelation in the third column of the chart. Some sample answers follow guide you in your discussion. Your students will undoubtedly find many other details to list.

Appearance	Bianca's face is red.	She is embarrassed or self-conscious.
Speech	"You are a fantastic speller."	She is a good sport.
Actions	She wipes her hands on her skirt.	She is nervous.
Private thoughts	She thinks her dark brown eyes are "boring."	She is not confident.
Others' reactions	Her dad gave her a thumbs-up, and her mom blew her a kiss.	She is loved by her family.

6. Save your class's work and make a copy for each student's writing folder.

body's Perfect!

Display *Nobody's Perfect!* on the SMART Board. Use the Screen Shade to conceal everything but the title and introduction. Share with students that authors often try to create characters readers will like and sympathize with. Use prompts to explore what that means. Ask: *What makes us like a person in real life? Must a story character be perfect in order for readers to like him or her? Why or why not?*

Note that everyone has flaws, even book characters. In fact, it is often a main character's flaw that makes for an interesting story! Point out that a main character's flaw is usually something readers can easily understand and forgive. Share some examples with the class, and let students share some examples from books they've read.

Book	Character	Flaw
Chocolate Fever (Robert Kimmel Smith)	Henry	Liking chocolate too much
The Mouse and the Motorcycle (Beverly Cleary)	Ralph	Not listening to his mother
"Goldilocks and the Three Bears"	Goldilocks	Being nosy
Chrysanthemum (Kevin Henkes)	Chrysanthemum	Being embarrassed by her name

Read the directions and review how a character's imperfection can sometimes lead to the main conflict or problem in the story. Use the examples that students cited earlier to illustrate. For example, Goldilocks's nosiness causes her to explore the bears' home—and fall asleep inside.

Open the Screen Shade to reveal the first picture and character sketch. Explain that students will read about this character, Allie, and think about how her flaw could lead to a problem for a story. Have students read the blurb and brainstorm story ideas for Allie. Have volunteers write or type the ideas in the text box.

Repeat with the remaining two character sketches. Have students list problems Tad and Cilenna might face that would lead to interesting narratives. For an exciting challenge, have students try to come up with a storyline or plot problem that involves at least two of the three characters.

Encourage students to use this technique when they need to come up with story ideas. Facilitate creativity by clipping photos of people from magazines or newspapers and placing them in a "Choose a Character" box you set up in your writing center. Students can select a photo, think of a character description, and imagine some related conflicts.

Save your class's work and make a copy for each student's writing folder.

Character Do's and Don'ts

1. Display *Character Do's and Don'ts* on the SMART Board. Explain that student will read a series of "tips" and decide if each one is a good way to create characters for a story. To respond to each statement, students will need to dr on what they have learned so far in this unit and use critical-thinking skills.

2. Read aloud the first statement and ask students to share whether they think it is a "Do" or a "Don't" for creating characters. Have students support their responses with reasons. After your discussion, invite a student to approach the SMART Board and touch the answer on which the class has agreed. If th student selects the correct answer, the button will spin. If the student selects the incorrect answer, no animation will occur.

3. Repeat this exercise with the remaining statements. Use the Understanding and Don'ts box below to discuss the thinking behind the answers.

Understanding Do's and Don'ts

1. **DO** choose one or two characters to be your main characters. One usually works best, though experienced authors can sometimes manage to develop two. A main character gives readers a person to focus on and connect with.

2. **DON'T** make your main character perfect. Remind students that we want our characters to seem real to our readers. Real people have imperfections and problems.

3. **DO** observe people to get ideas for characters. All writers use bits of people they know in their fictional characters. A writer might create a character with her uncle's bald head and her brother's interest in birds. Some authors call this the "spare parts" approach to creating characters. They build characters with all the spare parts (personalities, physical traits, etc.) they have noticed in various people.

4. **DON'T** make a character who looks, talks, and acts exactly like someone you know. That might make the person uncomfortable.

5. **DO** think about a character's appearance, personality, likes, and dislikes before starting a story. Explain to students that this is called a character sketch. Creating one helps a writer keep a character consistent—or the same— throughout the story. Without a character sketch, it would be easy to have a character eat peas in Chapter 1, then claim to be allergic to them in Chapter 4.

6. **DO** show readers what a main character is thinking and feeling. Remind students this is one of the things that distinguishes a main character from a secondary one. With a main character, we can see what's going on inside his or her head.

7. **DON'T** include as many characters as you can think of. Too large a cast of characters will only confuse readers and make it hard to follow the story. Instead, think of a few characters who are helpful to your story.

8. **DO** write dialogue for your characters. Remind students that dialogue is a great way to reveal information about the characters. As students will discover in the Developing Dialogue unit, dialogue also helps move a story along.

EXTENDED LEARNING

eating Characters: Your Turn!

Print and make copies of *Creating Characters: Your Turn!* for students. Display the Notebook page on the SMART Board. Distribute copies of the worksheets. Explain that students will complete this page on their own, either in class or for homework, to apply what they have learned about story characters.

Review the directions with students, explaining that they will create a brief character sketch of an original fictional character. Point out to students that they will be thinking about their character's:

- name and age
- appearance
- strong and weak qualities
- favorite and least favorite things
- main goal or motivation in life

Students will also be using their character sketch to generate some story ideas in which this character could star.

Once students have completed their sketches, invite volunteers to share their work with the class.

Hatching a Plot

Creating narrative problems will be no problem at all once your students ha
explored this series of Notebook pages! Students will learn how to build an
exciting plot complete with conflict, solution, and suspense.

OBJECTIVES

Students will be able to:

✓ Recognize that narrative plots have a beginning, middle, and end.

✓ Identify the main conflict or problem in a narrative plot.

✓ Distinguish between types of plot conflicts.

✓ Apply techniques for developing plot, including building suspense.

TIME

About 3–4 class periods for Unit 3 (allow 15–20 minutes per lesson)

MEETING THE STANDARDS

This lesson correlates with the following writing standards for grades 3 through (

• Students analyze the use of literary elements by an author,
including plot.

• Students compose stories with a beginning, middle, and end.

• Students understand and apply literary conflict.

GETTING READY

Before students arrive, have your SMART Board ready to go. Load the Writing
Lessons CD onto your host computer and copy the 3 SMART Plot Notebook file
onto your hard drive. Open the local file. The first interactive page, *What Is Plot?*
will appear on your SMART Board. If you wish, use your Screen Shade tool
to conceal the page until you are ready to begin.

What Is Plot?

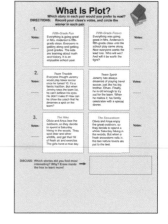

Display *What Is Plot?* on the SMART Board and read the page directions aloud. Explain that students are going to read two different versions of a story summary and decide which one sounds more interesting.

Have student volunteers read aloud the two versions of story number 1: *Fifth-Grade Fun* and *Fifth-Grade Fiasco.* Afterward, ask for a show of hands indicating which version of the story students prefer. Record the number of votes each version received on the line in the page margin. Invite a student to use the SMART pens or Creative Pens to circle the winning story summary.

Repeat the voting with stories 2 and 3. Again, record the number of votes each version received and circle the winning version. Discuss why students voted the way they did. Ask: *What was it about the story summary that caught your attention? Why was the other story not as interesting to you?*

If students have consistently voted for the story with the conflict (*Fifth-Grade Fiasco, Team Trouble,* and *The Snowstorm*), point out that you see a pattern in the student voting and challenge students to spot the pattern. Point out that most readers are drawn to stories with exciting problems or conflicts. Stories with no problems are boring!

Finally, invite a student volunteer to erase the background inside the box at the bottom of the page. A "secret" about plot will be revealed: Most narrative plots have a problem and a solution. To explore this concept further, have students name some plot problems from books they have read recently.

 TECH TIP

Whenever you use the SMART eraser, be sure to put it back in its spot when you are done. If you do not replace the eraser, the SMART Board will continue reading your next action as an erasure.

What's the Problem?

1. Display *What's the Problem?* on the SMART Board. Remind students that they have already learned that plot is usually centered on a problem, or conflict, and a solution. Now let them know that most plot problems fall into four categories. Have students read the description of each category on the chart.

PLOT CATEGORIES

- **Character against character:** Someone else causes a problem for the main character.

- **Character against nature:** A force of nature (weather, fire, etc.) causes a problem for the main character.

- **Character against self:** The main character is torn in two directions and must make a choice. Explain that this is sometimes called an *internal conflict*.

- **Character against society:** The main character disagrees with or lives in opposition to the rules or ideas of the community.

2. Explain that students will place examples of each type of conflict in the remaining columns of the chart. Point out that the examples are in text boxes surrounding the chart and can be dragged and dropped into position with a finger. Have a volunteer read aloud the first example on the top right. Invite him or her to name the kind of conflict the example represents, then drag and drop the text box to the appropriate spot on the chart.

3. Repeat with the remaining seven examples, until only the last column of the chart is empty. Explain that in this column, students will record their own examples of plot conflicts. Have students work in pairs to brainstorm an example for each category. Invite pairs to add their examples to the chart using the on-screen keyboard. Let students know that examples can be from actual books they have read, from movies, or from their imaginations.

4. Save your class's work and make a copy for each student's writing folder.

a Problem Solver!

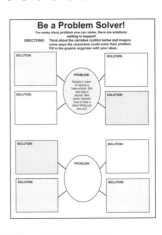

Have students recall some examples of plot problems from books they have read and ask if they can remember how each problem was solved. Guide students to understand that how the main character solves his or her problem is the meat, or substance, of a story.

Display *Be a Problem Solver!* on the SMART Board and read the page directions. Direct students' attention to the first idea web and read aloud the problem in the center oval.

Natalia's class is having a bike-a-thon. But she has a secret. She never learned how to ride a bike!

Explain that students should brainstorm as many creative solutions to that problem as they can. As students come up with possible solutions, invite them to record their ideas in the rectangles of the graphic organizer by using the SMART pens or the on-screen keyboard.

Once the class has recorded three or four possible solutions, discuss which solutions students think would work best if this were a real book. Challenge students to give reasons to support their opinions. Some considerations might include the following:

- It is not the ending you would expect at the beginning of the story. (Many readers like surprise endings!)

- It shows the main character taking control and solving the problem without adult intervention.

- It is realistic. (This problem appears to be an example of realistic fiction, so the solution should probably be realistic. Only in science fiction do space aliens save the day.)

- It helps the character change or grow. (An ending in which Natalia gets out of the bike-a-thon by playing sick would solve her immediate problem, but not her larger problem.)

Move on to the second idea web. Point out that this one is empty. It is up to students to generate a plot problem to put in the center oval. Elicit some suggestions from the class, then choose one you think will lend itself to several possible endings. Use the SMART pen or the on-screen keyboard to write it in the oval.

Have students describe and record possible endings for the problem on the graphic organizer. Again, have them pick the ending they would enjoy most if they were reading a book with this plot problem.

Save your class's work on the graphic organizers and make a copy for each student's writing folder.

TECH TIP

Is your writing not showing up on the screen? Try pushing a little harder with the SMART pen! Keep in mind that you will not damage the SMART Board by applying pressure with the pens.

Plot Parts, Part 1

1. Guide students to recall that plots have a problem and a solution. Explain th[at] as authors write story plots, they often describe problem and solution using [a] predictable pattern, or *formula*. Have students briefly share other formulas t[hey] know about (recipes, etc.), establishing that following a formula means usin[g] certain ingredients in a certain order.

2. Display *Plot Parts, Part 1* on the SMART Board. Point out the simple line diagram at the top of the page and explain that it represents the pattern ma[ny] plots follow. Ask students what they think the diagram looks like, then expl[ain] that most people think of plot pattern as a pyramid or mountain. This patte[rn] was first described thousands of years ago by the ancient Greek writer and philosopher Aristotle.

3. Have students read the names and descriptions of the five plot parts under [the] diagram. Using a finger, show how each text box can be dragged and dropp[ed] within the Notebook page. Explain that students will use deductive reasoni[ng] to place each descriptor in its correct spot on the diagram. Point out that th[e] text boxes should correspond to the black circles on the diagram line.

4. Have students take turns placing the text boxes around the diagram, then reread the plot parts to ensure they make sense.

5. Scroll down to the second part of the page. Explain that in this follow-up activity, students will see how a plot diagram works with a real story, "Goldilocks and the Three Bears." Point out that the plot diagram looks exac[tly] the same as the one at the top of the page.

6. Challenge students to place the text boxes describing parts of the fairy tale a[t] appropriate spots on the diagram. Explain that there are more text boxes tha[n] there are circles on the diagram. That means at least one plot part includes several events. Guide students to understand that this is true of most stories[. If] students have trouble with the activity, you may wish to point out that in thi[s] diagram, the rising action includes three separate events.

7. Save your class's work and make a copy for each student's writing folder.

If time has passed since students explored *Plot Parts, Part 1*, take a moment to review the five parts of a typical narrative plot: exposition, rising action, climax, falling action, resolution. Guide students to recall what happens in each part.

Display *Plot Parts, Part 2* on the SMART Board and read the directions for the page together. Explain that students will be reading a short story and identifying the five parts of its plot.

Before beginning, remind students how to change the ink color of a SMART pen. Simply pick up the pen, then click on the Properties tab on the left side of the board. Select the desired color from the palette.

Read the short story aloud all the way through. Then return to the beginning and use prompts to have students pick out and draw boxes around the five parts.

- *The beginning, or exposition, introduces the setting and characters and briefly tells us about the problem. Where is that part in this story? Let's draw a yellow box around it.* (Paragraphs 1 through 5)

- *The rising action tells how the characters begin trying to solve the problem. What part of this story tells us how Meg and her mom try to find Freddy? Let's draw an orange box around it.* (Paragraphs 6 and 7)

- *The climax is the exciting turning point—the spot when we see that things are going to change. Where in this story do we see that maybe we will find Freddy? Let's draw a red box around that part.* (Paragraph 8)

- *The falling action includes the steps that lead up to the resolution. What part of the story tells us what Meg and her mom did after Meg spotted the trail? Let's draw a purple box around that part.* (Paragraph 9)

- *The resolution tells us how the problem gets solved and how things get back to normal for the characters. Which paragraphs do that in this story? Let's draw a blue box around it.* (Paragraphs 10 through 12)

Save your class's work and make a copy for each student's writing folder.

Build Suspense!

1. Engage students by inviting them to recall books they could not put down or movies that had them on the edge of their seats. Discuss what it was about the book or movie that so captured their attention. Possible responses might include: *I couldn't wait to find out what was going to happen next. It kept getting more and more exciting. I was afraid I would miss something. I wanted to see how would end.* Explain that this element is called *suspense.* Ask students if they a familiar with the word. Explain that while we usually think of suspense as a ingredient in mysteries, it is an important part of many kinds of story plots.

2. Display *Build Suspense!* on the SMART Board. Use your Screen Shade to con the circled examples on the right side of the page. Explain that good writers have some techniques, or tricks, for building suspense in a story plot. These include giving a time limit for solving the problem, having the character wonder aloud what's about to happen, describing clues and events in threes and using foreshadowing. Read about these techniques in the column on th left, asking students if they recognize any of the techniques from books they have read.

3. Open your Screen Shade to reveal the examples on the right. Invite one student at a time to approach the SMART Board and use a favorite Creative to draw a line matching a suspense technique to its corresponding example

4. Direct students' attention to the Discuss question at the bottom of the Notebook page. Have students offer examples of how they could use some of the suspense techniques they have learned to develop the plot about the missing field-trip money. Sample responses include the following:

> - **Racing the Clock:** Let readers know the trip is set to happen in one week!
>
> - **Asking Questions:** Have Daniel wonder, "Who could have gotten into the desk?"
>
> - **Using the Magic of 3:** Rule out two suspects before finding the culprit.
>
> - **Giving a Sneak Peek:** Have Daniel spot something that ends up being a clue. For example, if someone's two-year-old brother took the money, Daniel might see a stuffed toy near the desk.

5. Save your class's work and make a copy for each student's writing folder.

t and Theme

Tell students they will explore one more aspect of plot before developing story plots of their own. Explain that some stories leave readers with a certain message or feeling about the world. This is called *theme*. Explain that authors rarely come out and tell readers the theme of a story. Instead, they let you come up with the theme on your own by thinking about what happened in the story.

Display *Plot and Theme* on the SMART Board and read the directions together. Discuss the "Cinderella" example and ask students if they can think of the themes of any stories they have read.

Read the first story summary and talk about possible themes. To identify theme, instruct students to ask themselves: *What lesson does the main character learn in the story? Is it something useful or important for me to remember, too?*

When students have identified a possible theme for the first story summary, use your SMART Eraser to erase inside the box on the right of the story summary. One possible theme will be revealed. Discuss whether your class's ideas matched the theme inside the box, pointing out that stories can have more than one theme.

Repeat the discussion activity with the second story summary, then erase inside the box to reveal that story's theme.

EXTENDED LEARNING

tching a Plot: Your Turn!

Print and make copies of *Hatching a Plot: Your Turn!* for students. Display the Notebook page on the SMART Board. Distibute copies of the worksheet. Explain that students will complete this page on their own, either in class or for homework, to apply what they have learned about story plots. The activity will also draw on students' knowledge of setting and characters.

Review the directions with students, explaining that they will use a picture prompt to plan an original story plot. Remind students to:

- introduce the characters, setting, and problem in the exposition, or beginning.
- include rising action that tells how the problem grows worse.
- include an exciting climax, or turning point.
- reveal how the problem ultimately gets resolved.

Students should plan their plots using the prompts on the worksheet. If time allows, and you wish, have students write a draft of their story on a separate sheet of paper.

Once students have completed their plot plans, invite volunteers to share their work with the class.

Developing Dialogue

Early attempts at writing dialogue are often plagued with pitfalls. Speakers are left unidentified, conversations go on forever, and punctuation is missin in action. Use this series of SMART Notebook pages to help students begin writing dialogue that dazzles!

OBJECTIVES

Students will be able to:

✓ Understand that dialogue moves a story along and gives clues about characters.

✓ Write dialogue that sounds authentic and interesting.

✓ Correctly punctuate and format dialogue.

TIME

About 3–4 class periods for Unit 4 (allow 15–20 minutes per lesson)

MEETING THE STANDARDS

This lesson correlates with the following writing standards for grades 3 through (

• Students understand how literary elements and techniques are used to convey meaning.

• Students use a range of narrative devices, including dialogue.

• Students punctuate dialogue with quotation marks, commas, and end marks.

GETTING READY

Before students arrive, have your SMART Board ready to go. Load the Writing Lessons CD onto your host computer and copy the 4 SMART Dialogue Noteboo file onto your hard drive. Open the local file. The first interactive page, *Reasons* V *Talk*, will appear on your SMART Board. If you wish, use your Screen Shade tool to conceal the page until you are ready to begin.

asons We Talk

Display *Reasons We Talk*. Launch your lesson by noting that characters in stories often talk with one another, just like real people do. Guide students to understand that this is known as *dialogue*. Then activate prior knowledge by exploring real-life dialogue. Invite your students to recall conversations they have had today at home or at school. Ask volunteers to share snippets from those conversations and discuss the reason or purpose for each one. Reasons might include:

- To get information
- To give information
- To share feelings
- To make plans
- To pass time
- To make introductions
- To give instructions
- To share opinions

Record both reasons and brief dialogue examples on the *Reasons We Talk* graphic organizer. If you wish, have students use the SMART pens or on-screen keyboard to write or type in the examples themselves. (Although you will not directly address the use of quotation marks until later in this unit, model their use by including them as you write an example of dialogue inside the organizer.)

Don't worry about exhausting all possibilities! Record enough examples to give students a sense of the many reasons we talk with one another. When a student offers an example of speech that matches a reason the class has already discussed, point out that the new example is similar to the previously discussed example.

Explain that characters in stories have conversations for many of the same reasons real people do. However, they do far less talking than we do in real life! To help students understand why dialogue is limited in a narrative, have them imagine writing down every conversation they had for a whole day. Discuss: *How much space would it take you to write it all down? Would all of it be interesting to other people?*

Guide students to understand that a writer tries to keep readers interested in his or her story. For that reason, the writer includes only those pieces of dialogue that help the story and leaves out unnecessary or boring conversations.

Save your class's work and make a copy for each student's writing folder.

INTERACTIVE LEARNING

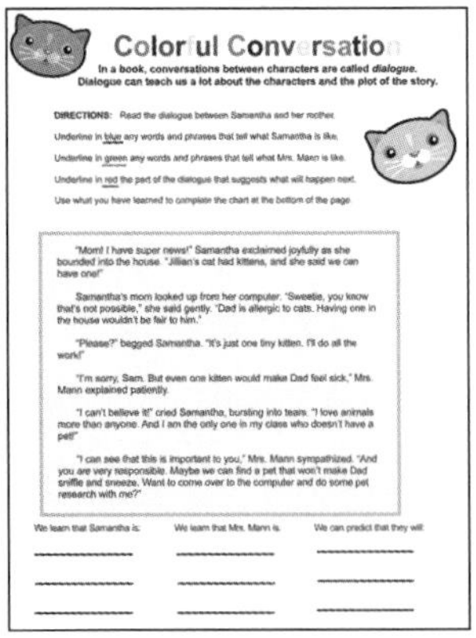

Colorful Conversation

In a book, conversations between characters are called *dialogue*. Dialogue can teach us a lot about the characters and the plot of the story.

DIRECTIONS: Read the dialogue between Samantha and her mother.

Underline in blue any words and phrases that tell what Samantha is like.

Underline in green any words and phrases that tell what Mrs. Mann is like.

Underline in red the part of the dialogue that suggests what will happen next.

Use what you have learned to complete the chart at the bottom of the page.

"Mom! I have super news!" Samantha exclaimed joyfully as she bounded into the house. "Jillian's cat had kittens, and she said we can have one!"

Samantha's mom looked up from her computer. "Sweetie, you know that's not possible," she said gently. "Dad is allergic to cats. Having one in the house wouldn't be fair to him."

"Please?" begged Samantha. "It's just one tiny kitten. I'll do all the work!"

"I'm sorry, Sam. But even one kitten would make Dad feel sick," Mrs. Mann explained patiently.

"I can't believe it!" cried Samantha, bursting into tears. "I love animals more than anyone. And I am the only one in my class who doesn't have a pet!"

"I can see that this is important to you," Mrs. Mann sympathized. "And you are very responsible. Maybe we can find a pet that won't make Dad sniffle and sneeze. Want to come over to the computer and do some pet research with me?"

We learn that Samantha is:	We learn that Mrs. Mann is:	We can predict that they will:

Colorful Conversation

1. Use prompts to introduce the two main ways dialogue can help a story—tel about characters and moving the plot forward. You might say the following.

   - *Dialogue can tell us more about the characters. For example, let's imagine that I am a substitute teacher who just walked in for the first time, and I say, "Everyone get your books out right now. I won't put up with any nonsense in this classroom." What do my words tell you about me? What does my tone of voice tell you about me?*

   - *Dialogue can give clues about a problem the characters in the story will face or reveal how the characters might solve that problem. What do we call the problem and solution in a story?* (Plot)

2. Display *Colorful Conversation* on the SMART Board. Explain that the class wi read aloud a dialogue between two characters. Then they will go back and underline parts of the dialogue that tell about the characters and the plot. H volunteers read the short dialogue aloud, then use the SMART pens and wo with students to mark the passage as follows. To avoid confusion, finish one instruction before moving on to the next.

   - Underline in blue any words or phrases that tell what Samantha is like.
   - Underline in green any words and phrases that tell what Mrs. Mann is like.
   - Underline in red the part of the dialogue that suggests what will happen next.

3. Discuss what the dialogue revealed about the characters and plot. Use these findings to fill in the graphic organizer at the bottom of the Notebook page. Students can use the SMART pens to write directly on the lines.

4. Save your class's work and make a copy for each student's writing folder.

TECH TIP

Did you goof up? Don't worry! Notebook offers a backtracking tool to let you click back to before it all happened! Simply click on the blue reverse arrow to undo your last action. You may repeat to undo several actions. And if you change your mind, just click the forward arrow to redo the action.

Said, She Said

Tell students they are going to practice crafting dialogue that sounds natural and moves a story along. Display *He Said, She Said* on the SMART Board and direct students' attention to the picture. Elicit ideas about what might be going on between the two characters.

Have students work in pairs for several minutes to jot down a brief dialogue between the two characters. Use prompts, such as:

- *How do the two characters know one another?*
- *What has happened?*
- *What are they saying to each other?*

When students have finished, invite two partners to approach the SMART Board. Have them stand on either side of the screen (next to the speech bubbles) and role-play their dialogue. Write their remarks into the speech bubbles, or access your on-screen keyboard to type in the remarks. (You may wish to have students type or write the dialogue themselves.) Be sure to use quotation marks and other appropriate punctuation.

Discuss what the pair's dialogue reveals about the individual characters in the photo and the plot of the "story." Point out words or phrases that make the dialogue sound authentic.

Invite other pairs to share their dialogues with the class in similar fashion. Celebrate that different pairs steered the dialogue in different directions and gave different personalities to the characters. Remind students that original ideas and a strong voice are central to good writing.

Save a favorite dialogue and make a copy for each student's writing folder.

ok Who's Talking!

Display *Look Who's Talking!* on the SMART Board. Explain that writers use phrases called *speech tags* to show their readers which character is speaking. Offer a few examples, such as "Tim asked," "remarked Gloria," or "Mr. Newman announced."

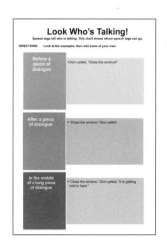

Direct students to look at the chart on the Notebook page. Use the chart to demonstrate that speech tags can appear at the beginning of a piece of dialogue, at the end of a piece of dialogue, or, when a piece of dialogue includes more than one sentence, right in the middle.

Have student volunteers read aloud the examples. Then ask for other examples and have students write or type the new examples into the graphic organizer.

Explain that in stories, it is more common to see speech tags at the end or in the middle of a piece of dialogue than at the beginning. That helps the author avoid starting multiple sentences with the same phrase (such as "John said"). Discuss how that improves sentence fluency, an important writing trait.

Save your class's work and make a copy for each student's writing folder.

Put "Said" to Bed!

1. Point out to students that the word *said* is often overused in narrative dialogues. While it is sometimes precisely the right verb to use, a more interesting replacement can frequently be found. To illustrate, share the following two sets of quotes with students:

> *"Give me five more minutes,"* Fiona said.
>
> *"Give me five more minutes,"* Fiona mumbled.
>
> *"Good morning,"* said the teacher.
>
> *"Good morning,"* the teacher chirped.

Discuss how the verbs in these speech tags affect the dialogue. While *said* d[...] the job, the other verbs give additional information about the speaker and make the writing livelier. Point out that specific word choice is one of the tr[...] of good writing.

2. Display *Put "Said" to Bed* on the SMART Board. Have students read aloud th[...] passage on the SMART Board. Explain that the class is going to work togeth[...] to revise the passage, replacing *said* with more interesting and precise verbs[...]

3. Take a moment to demonstrate the "drag and drop" feature of Notebook. Fi[...] the word *said* in the story and double click the word with your finger. Drag[...] to another spot on the page and then put it back in place. Explain that stud[...] will "drag and drop" the word *said* to the bed at the bottom of the page. The[...] are enough spots on the bed for each *said* in the story.

4. Reread the story, pausing each time you come to *said*. Have a student volun[...] drag and drop the word onto the bed. Notice that a blank space will appear[...] its spot in the story. Elicit possible substitutions that make sense in the cont[...] then choose a class favorite and type or write it in. (Most of your new verbs[...] will be longer than *said*. You may need to use an editing caret and write the[...] new words slightly above the line of original text.)

5. Repeat until the whole passage has been revised. While the various *said* substitutions are still fresh in students' heads, move quickly to the next less[...]

6. Save your class's work and make a copy for each student's writing folder.

tead of Said . . .

Display *Instead of Said . . .* on the SMART Board. Remind students they have already explored many alternatives to the verb *said*. Explain that now they are going to make a mini-poster of alternatives to display in the classroom and/or store in their writing folders.

To begin, explore the verbs that already appear on the page. Tell students that they are going to use the Magic Pen to highlight which verb to use in different writing situations. With this pen, students can circle a portion of a page to shine a "spotlight" on that spot. Demonstrate by clicking on the Magic Pen with your finger, then using your finger to circle the title on the page.

After the demonstration, read the following prompts aloud. After each prompt, invite a student volunteer to circle the appropriate verb on the screen with the Magic Pen.

- *The kids made a big mess, and Mom wanted them to clean up right away. How did she tell them?* (ordered)

- *Sadie had a secret to tell Pam. How did she tell her?* (whispered)

- *Your big brother accidentally stepped on your toe. How did you say "ouch"?* (yelped)

- *Max stopped at the deli to ask if they have any turkey. Which verb would you use to show how Max asked?* (inquired)

Older students may enjoy coming up with writing situations for the remaining verbs.

Have students add their own fun verbs to the page. Point out that since this will serve as a mini-poster, the words need to be large and legible. Have students observe as you increase the point size. Then invite them to help you choose a font and color for each verb that mirrors the mood and meaning of the word. (Go to the Text tool on your Notebook toolbar for text fonts and colors.) Younger students may prefer to add verbs to the poster by writing them with the SMART pens and changing the color and line style to match the verb's mood.

When you are through, print out a copy of the mini-poster to display in the classroom and make a copy for each student.

💡 TECH TIP

.ost a tool? If you need a tool (such as the Magic Pen) but can't find it on your
oolbar, just right-click on your toolbar. A master menu of tools will appear on
creen. Drag and drop the tool of your choice onto your toolbar.

Punctuating Dialogue

Punctuating Dialogue

1. Display *Punctuating Dialogue* on the SMART Board. Explain to students that knowing how to punctuate and paragraph dialogue correctly will improve t clarity of their writing. Tell them that in this lesson, they will study a model observe how a real author formats and punctuates a passage of dialogue.

2. Draw students' attention to the screen and explain that the passage is an excerpt from *Twister on Tuesday,* a book in the Magic Tree House series by Mary Pope Osborne. Have students read the dialogue and look for patterns punctuation, capitalization, and paragraphing. Remind them that this aspec writing is known as *mechanics.*

3. Have students use the SMART pens to mark the text, following the direction on the right side of the page.

   - Circle quotation marks in **blue**.
   - Circle commas in **red**.
   - Circle periods, question marks, and exclamation points in **green**.
   - Circle all words that are capitalized inside the quotation marks in **black**.
   - Use a **yellow** checkmark to show where a new paragraph begins.

4. Use prompts to discuss any rules and patterns students notice. For exampl you might ask the following:

   - *What marks does the writer use to show that these are a character's exact words? Where do these marks go?* (Quotation marks go before and after the exact words.)
   - *Do sentence enders like periods, exclamation points, and question marks go inside or outside the quotation marks?* (Inside)
   - *What punctuation mark does the writer often use to separate the dialogue from the speech tag?* (A comma)
   - *Why do you think the writer made a new paragraph here?* (To show that a new character was speaking)

5. Record the rules for punctuating dialogue by writing or typing them into th chart at the bottom of the page. Your chart should include rules such as the following:

   > - Use quotation marks before and after a piece of dialogue.
   > - If the speech tag goes before the dialogue, it is followed by a comma.
   > - If the dialogue goes before the speech tag, a comma, exclamation point, or question mark goes inside the quotation marks.
   > - A piece of dialogue begins with a capital letter.
   > - Start a new paragraph each time the speaker changes.

6. Save your class's work and make a copy for each student's writing folder.

veloping Dialogue: Your Turn!

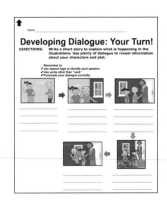

Print and make copies of *Developing Dialogue: Your Turn!* for students. Display the Notebook page on the SMART Board. Distribute copies of the worksheet. Explain that students will complete this page on their own, either in class or for homework, to apply what they have learned about dialogue.

Review the directions with students, explaining that they will write dialogue for a mini-narrative based on the storyboard. Remind students to:

- use dialogue to reveal character traits and move the plot along.
- use speech tags.
- consider exciting alternatives to *said*.
- correctly punctuate and paragraph the dialogue.

Once students have completed their sketches, invite volunteers to share their work with the class.

Organizing Ideas

By now, your students have learned how to generate wonderfully original settings, characters, plots, and dialogue. Use the Notebook pages in this unit to help them tie it all together!

OBJECTIVES

Students will be able to:

✓ Write strong narrative beginnings and endings.

✓ Write paragraphs focusing on a central idea.

✓ Omit unnecessary or uninteresting details from a narrative.

✓ Use transition words to sequence events in a story.

TIME

About 3–4 class periods for Unit 5 (allow 15–20 minutes per lesson)

MEETING THE STANDARDS

This lesson correlates with the following writing standards for grades 3 through 6

• Students identify and use effective leads and strong endings.

• Students organize writing to convey a central idea.

• Students organize information logically.

• Students use techniques such as signal words to clarify organizational structure.

GETTING READY

Before students arrive, have your SMART Board ready to go. Load the Writing Lessons CD onto your host computer and copy the 5 SMART Organization Notebook file onto your hard drive. Open the local file. The first interactive page *Noticing Organization,* will appear on your SMART Board. If you wish, use your Screen Shade tool ⬚ to conceal the page until you are ready to begin.

...ticing Organization

Remind students that they have learned all about the ingredients of a good story: setting, characters, plot, and dialogue. Explain that now they are going to explore some ways to put those ingredients together in an organized narrative. To tap into prior knowledge, briefly review with students the meaning of the word *organized*. Ask students to describe an organized classroom and a disorganized classroom. Some sample responses are listed below.

Noticing Organization reproducible page

Organized

Things are in the right places.

Things appear neat and orderly.

Things may be labeled.

No junk is lying around.

Disorganized

Nothing is where it is supposed to be.

Things look messy.

Nothing is clearly labeled.

Trash and junk are all around.

Discuss with students how they feel upon entering a messy, disorganized room. (Chances are they want to leave as soon as possible.) Explain that readers have a similar reaction to a disorganized story. Good writers work hard to organize their stories so they can get and hold readers' attention.

Display *Noticing Organization* on the SMART Board and read the page directions aloud. Explain that students are going to read two different versions of a short story. The first is a rough draft, and the second is a revision. Advise students to look for ways the writer revised the story to improve its organization.

Read aloud the rough draft of the story in the text box on the left. Pause to ask students what they thought of it. Ask: *Does the story grab and hold your attention? Does it make sense? Why not?*

Next, read aloud the revised version of the story. Afterward, ask students what they notice about the story's organization, using prompts like the ones below.

- *How did the writer change the beginning? Why is the new one better?*
- *How are the paragraphs different in the revision?*
- *Can you find a spot where the writer changed the order of events? Why do you think he or she made this change?*
- *In the rough draft, did you notice any details that didn't belong? What happened to them in the revision?*
- *How did the writer change the ending? Why is the new one better?*

Summarize students' comments in the graphic organizer at the bottom of the page.

TECH TIP

Don't waste space! Maximize your screen space by clicking on the Full Screen icon . The Notebook page you are viewing will expand to fill the screen, making it easier for the class to read. When you are finished with the page, simply click on the icon again to return to a standard screen format.

Bright Beginnings

1. Display *Bright Beginnings* on the SMART Board. (Students will enjoy watchin the idea wheel spin as you enter the Notebook page!) Remind students of the class discussion about organized and disorganized rooms. Ask: *If a room looks like a disaster from the doorway, do you want to go in?* Guide students to understand that good story organization begins right at the beginning, with strong story opener. Explain that in this lesson, students will learn some wa to craft strong openings.

2. Read aloud the introduction and the descriptions of the five types of story beginnings. Emphasize that the ideas on this wheel are not the only ways to begin a story. Explain that as students notice other ways, they can add them the wheel.

3. Read aloud the story beginnings listed on page 43. After you read each one, invite a student volunteer to approach the SMART Board and circle the corresponding technique on the wheel. Have the student use the Magic Pen so that the featured technique will be spotlighted. When you finish discussi each example, click on the red *X* to close the Magic Pen spotlight.

4. If you wish, continue the activity using picture books or chapter books from your classroom library. If students identify additional techniques for starting story, use the SMART pens to add these techniques to the wheel.

5. Save your class's work and make a copy for each student's writing folder.

SOME STORY BEGINNINGS

From the Mixed-Up Files of Mrs. Basil E. Frankweiler by E. L. Konigsburg

Claudia knew that she could never pull off the old-fashioned kind of running away. That is, running away in the heat of anger with a knapsack on her back. Therefore, she decided that her leaving home would not be just running from somewhere but would be running to somewhere.

Technique: Jump right in

In the Year of the Boar and Jackie Robinson by Bette Bao Lord

In the Year of the Dog, 4645, there lived halfway across the world from New York, a girl called Sixth Cousin. Otherwise known as Bandit.

Technique: Either introduce a character or set the scene

Polar Bears Past Bedtime by Mary Pope Osborne

Whoo. The strange sound came from outside the open window.

Technique: Use sound effects

More Perfect Than the Moon by Patricia MacLachlan

Summer was cool and wet, and the barnyard was muddy. It was like spring left over.

Technique: Set the scene

Charlotte's Web by E. B. White

"Where's Papa going with that ax?" said Fern to her mother as they were setting the table for breakfast.

Technique: Share dialogue

Alexander, Who Used to Be Rich Last Sunday by Judith Viorst

It isn't fair that my brother Anthony has two dollars and three quarters and one dime and seven nickels and eighteen pennies.

Technique: Jump right in

Henry Huggins by Beverly Cleary

Henry Huggins was in the third grade. His hair looked like a scrubbing brush and most of his grown-up front teeth were in. He lived with his mother and father in a square white house on Klickitat Street.

Technique: Introduce a character

Put It in Order

1. Display *Put It in Order* on the SMART Board and read the page directions. U prompts to talk about the importance of putting ideas in an order that make sense.

   - *What if I told you a story about losing my favorite bracelet, but I forgot to tell you that it was at the beach until I was at the end of the story?*

   - *Would my story be confusing? Why?*

   Guide students to understand that when we revise stories, one thing we do to check that the story is told in a logical order.

2. Have students read aloud the story sentences in the colored boxes. Have volunteers sequence the events by dragging and dropping the boxes onto th timeline. Allow students to continue moving the boxes around until they are confident that the story is sequenced properly.

3. Read the story aloud. Then use the discussion prompt at the bottom of the page to talk about clues students used to put the events in order.

4. Save your class's work and make a copy for each student's writing folder.

Put It in Order

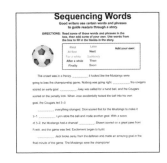

Display *Sequencing Words* on the SMART Board and read aloud the introductory material. Point out that writers use sequencing words like the ones in the box to show readers the order in which things happen.

Challenge students to think of other sequencing words and phrases. (If you wish, allow pairs of students to skim books from your classroom library to identify other sequencing words.) Add the new words and phrases to the box. Some possibilities are listed below.

Some Additional Sequencing Words

First	Earlier	Prior to
Second	During	Following
Third	Now	Immediately
When	While	Afterward

Read aloud the short story on the Notebook page, pausing each time you encounter a blank. Explain that each blank represents a missing sequencing word. Read through the story again. This time, invite student volunteers to approach the SMART Board and drag an appropriate sequencing word or phrase from the box to each blank line. Guide students to understand that in many cases, more than one word will make sense. Words may be (but do not need to be) used twice.

Read the story again, this time with the sequencing words in place. Ask students to think about how the sequencing words help readers. (They act as road signs or guides, putting events into correct context.) Point out that sequencing words often appear at the very beginning of a sentence.

Save your class's work and make a copy for each student's writing folder. Remind students to consult the list of sequencing words whenever they write narratives.

Puzzling Paragraphs

1. Review what students know about paragraphs. Remind them that a paragra[ph] is a group of sentences that belong together because they relate to the same main idea. Tell students that breaking a story into paragraphs is one way of organizing text for readers.

2. Display *Puzzling Paragraphs* on the SMART Board. Read the directions and ke[y] for the page together. Explain that students will read an excerpt from a short story and break it into two separate paragraphs. They will also identify details [in] those paragraphs that do not belong because they do not relate to the main id[ea].

3. Read the excerpt aloud. Invite students to tell where they think each paragr[aph] begins and ends. Invite a volunteer to mark each paragraph beginning with [a] paragraph symbol ¶. (Note that this symbol appears on the Key.) Discuss ho[w] students decided where to break the text and identify the main idea of each paragraph:

   • *Paragraph 1 is mainly about the physical signs that Hannah is nervous.*

   • *Paragraph 2 is mainly about the reason Hannah is nervous.*

4. Reread each paragraph. This time, have students identify details that are not closely related to the central idea of the paragraph. Explain that unnecessary details like these can distract and confuse readers. As students identify each unnecessary detail, have a volunteer click on that detail with a finger. If it is an unrelated or unnecessary detail, it will temporarily fly off the page. Wher[e it] returns to its spot on the screen, have students use the red SMART pen to d[raw] a delete line through it.

5. Reread the text once more, pausing between paragraphs and leaving out the irrelevant details. Discuss how the clarity of the writing has improved. Expla[in] that students should do similar revisions to their own writing to improve organization.

6. Save your class's work and make a copy for each student's writing folder.

ppy Endings

Activate prior knowledge by asking students to recall the endings of some of their favorite books. Have students describe the role of the ending in their own words. Responses may include:

> • It wraps everything up.
>
> • It shows that everyone gets back to normal.
>
> • It shows that the main problem is over.

Guide students to understand that endings should leave readers feeling satisfied.

Tell students that developing writers make two common mistakes when writing endings. Some end their stories too soon, before the conflict is fully resolved. This leaves readers full of questions. Others let their stories drag on for far too long, boring readers. Explain that students are going to take a look at one example of each problem.

Display *Happy Endings* on the SMART Board. Use your Screen Shade to conceal Part 2 at the bottom of the Notebook page while you direct students' attention to Part 1. Together, read the instructions for this part, then read aloud the short story about the fox and the goat. When you finish, ask students what they thought of the ending. Discuss where the story should have ended and why the extra details detracted from the narrative. Invite a student volunteer to clone the stop sign at the top of the page. Have the student drag the stop sign to the spot where the story should end.

Open your Screen Shade to reveal Part 2. Read the story aloud. Explain that this story has the opposite problem from the story in Part 1. It ends too suddenly, before the plot is resolved. Encourage students to describe endings that they think would satisfactorily resolve the story. Record their ideas in the space provided, using the SMART pens or on-screen keyboard.

Save your class's work and make a copy for each student's writing folder.

TECH TIP

To clone the stop sign, click on the image and touch the downward arrow that appears in the upper right, then scroll down to Clone.

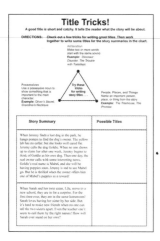

Title Tricks!

1. Remind students that although the title of a story is the first thing a reader reads, it is very often the last thing a writer writes. That's because the title should reflect the most important idea in a story. Invite students to share with the class some of their favorite story titles from picture books and novels they have read. Let students know that they are going to learn some tricks for writing their own effective titles.

2. Display *Title Tricks!* on the SMART Board and read the introductory material together. Read and discuss the three techniques for writing titles. Explain to students that these are not the only ways to write story titles.

3. Direct students' attention to the chart at the bottom of the page and read aloud the first story summary. Have students work in pairs or small groups to think of engaging titles for the story. Remind students that they may use the techniques from the triangle at the top of the page. Emphasize that titles should be short, catchy and should convey something important about the story.

4. Have students use the SMART pens to add their suggested titles to the chart. Once all groups have had a chance to add their titles, discuss what you like about each title. Vote on a class favorite, then have a student volunteer use the Shape Recognition tool to draw a circle around the selected title. Repeat with the second story summary.

5. Save your class's work and make a copy for each student's writing folder.

 **TECH TIP**

If students have trouble reaching the SMART toolbar at the top of the screen, click on the up-and-down arrow on the right end of your toolbar to move it to the bottom. Click on the arrow again to return the toolbar to the top.

EXTENDED LEARNING

Organizing Ideas: Your Turn!

1. Print and make copies of *Organizing Ideas: Your Turn!* for students. Display the Notebook page on the SMART Board. Explain that this checklist sums up all the important aspects of story organization that students have learned about this unit. Students will use the checklist to check and revise the organization of their own stories.

2. Review the directions with students, explaining that they will check each aspect of organization in their stories, then use the "Ways to Improve" areas to record ideas about how to improve the story's organization.

3. Distribute copies of the page to students. Have students complete the checklist each time they finish a story. If you wish, have students check their own story organization, then trade stories with a partner. Partners can evaluate one another's stories using the same checklist.